THE NATIONAL TRUST

Investigating FAMILY HISTORY

By Alison Honey
(With thanks to my personal genealogist – my father)

Illustrated by Pete Serjeant

Contents

Whose family?

How much do you know about your family and ancestors? You probably know about your parents and grandparents, but can you go back any further? This book shows how you can trace the personal history of families who lived or live in National Trust houses you visit, but it will also give you clues on how to find out more about your own family history.

Most of the families talked about in this book have well-documented histories, and tended to stay in the same house or at least in the same area for generations, leaving many clues for us to find out more. In this way it is relatively easy to trace their story through their home, their portraits, their belongings and the monuments which they left behind.

Pride and pedigrees

For thousands of years people of all cultures around the world have been fascinated by their ancestors and have wanted to find out more. Experts in tracing families back through generations are called genealogists – this word comes from two Greek words meaning 'family' and 'science'. Most people who use these experts are trying to establish their pedigree or family tree. Pedigree comes from two Latin words, 'pes' and 'grus', which together mean crane's foot and looked like the shape of a symbol used on early family trees.

Some of the early pedigrees were drawn up in the Middle Ages by monks and were beautifully illustrated. Many are much more than a list of names and show pictures of events or people relevant to the family.

Pass it on

In early civilisations people passed information on by word of mouth and this is how the first family trees descended from generation to generation. At the crowning ceremony of the ancient Scottish kings it was the royal bard's duty to recite a whole list of the new king's descendants off by heart. Because there is no written evidence of these spoken pedigrees we can't tell whether they were accurate or not.

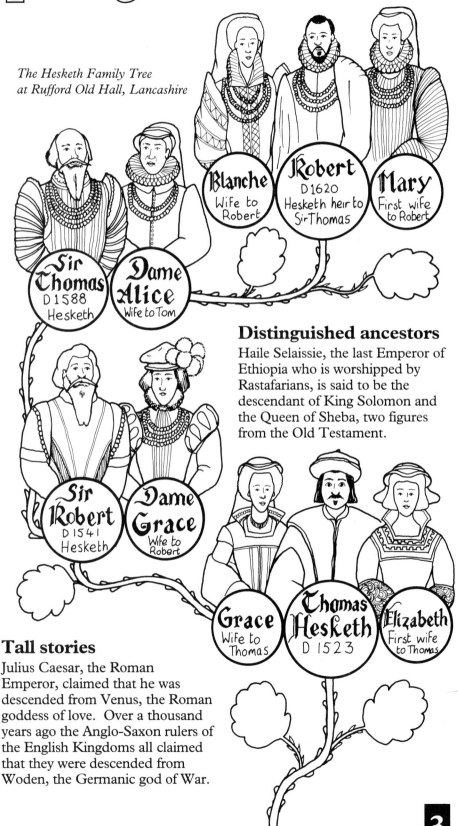

The Hesketh Family Tree at Rufford Old Hall, Lancashire

Blanche — Wife to Robert

Robert — D 1620 Hesketh heir to Sir Thomas

Mary — First wife to Robert

Sir Thomas — D 1588 Hesketh

Dame Alice — Wife to Tom

Sir Robert — D 1541 Hesketh

Dame Grace — Wife to Robert

Grace — Wife to Thomas

Thomas Hesketh — D 1523

Elizabeth — First wife to Thomas

Distinguished ancestors

Haile Selaissie, the last Emperor of Ethiopia who is worshipped by Rastafarians, is said to be the descendant of King Solomon and the Queen of Sheba, two figures from the Old Testament.

Tall stories

Julius Caesar, the Roman Emperor, claimed that he was descended from Venus, the Roman goddess of love. Over a thousand years ago the Anglo-Saxon rulers of the English Kingdoms all claimed that they were descended from Woden, the Germanic god of War.

Back to the Ark

Queen Elizabeth II's family tree can be traced back accurately to the early ninth century. However, if the monks who were responsible for writing down these pedigrees are to be believed, our present queen is descended from the Biblical character, Noah.

Ancestors for all

So far we've been talking about royalty and the upper levels of society, but after 1100, changes in English law meant that poorer people were also interested in identifying who their ancestors were. If they could prove that they were not villeins, a type of servant tied to the land, they were free to move around the country.

Domesday

It was also around this time that the greatest written record was undertaken in England – Domesday Book. This survey was ordered by William the Conqueror who had sailed across from Normandy in 1066 and conquered Harold, the English king, at the battle of Hastings. William wanted to find out as much as possible about his new lands so ordered his clerks to record the name of each place, who held it before 1066 and who held it after the conquest, how large it was, how many people lived there and what class of people they were. Domesday tells us a lot about the land but not so much about individuals, for the one thing William was keen to know was how much rent he could earn.

Spelling tests

By 1500 people from all levels of society were beginning to feature in documents recording births, marriages and deaths. The spelling of names on these registers changed from document to document as it was left to individual monks, who were often the only members of the community who could read and write, to decide how to spell each name.

Recorded for life

Since 1801 in England and Wales (since 1761 in Scotland) there has been a census every ten years. If you were in Britain on 21 and 22 April 1991 you will be recorded on the latest census. This is a survey which records every person in each household, their age, place of birth and occupation. After one hundred years the censuses become available to the public and are very useful documents for people tracing their family history.

Name of Street	Name and Surname	Relation to head of Family	Rank or Occupation
96 New Bond St	Emma Owen	Wife	Milliner
	Robert Owen	Head	Merchant
	John Smith	Servant	
	Alice Jones	Servant	
	Mary Owen	Daur	
	Charles Owen	Son	

Castle Drogo, Devon

Finding your roots

Julius Drew made his fortune by opening a shop called the 'Home and Colonial Stores' in London in 1883. With his new wealth he set about establishing himself as an English country gentleman. His elder brother consulted a genealogist who told the two brothers what they wanted to hear – that they were descendants of the ancient Drewe family in Devon. Julius added an 'e' to the end of his surname and then bought the Drewe family house. The researcher also claimed that the Drewe family was descended from Drogo, a Norman baron who had come over with William the Conqueror in 1066, and whose descendant, Drogo de Teigne, had given his name to a village in Devon, now known as Drewsteignton, in the twelfth century. With his enormous wealth Julius employed one of the best-known architects of the day, Sir Edwin Lutyens, to build a modern country house on a hill at Drewsteignton and named it Castle Drogo after his long-lost ancestor.

The language of heraldry

Heraldry developed in the twelfth century as a means of quick identification for heralds who had the job of reporting deaths and injuries of knights in battle. It was also important for knights who wore full suits of armour to be able to identify each other in the height of battle to check they were fighting the enemy, not someone from their own side! So knights started decorating their shields and surcoats (clothing worn over the armour) to distinguish themselves from others.

A long story

To begin with the symbols were quite simple and tended to be geometric designs or paintings of animals or birds connected with bravery and strength, such as the lion or eagle. King Richard the Lionheart, who took part in the Crusades of the twelfth century, used a red shield decorated with three gold leopards or lions and this has been part of the English royal family's shield ever since. As more and more knights adopted arms, it became necessary to compile a list of symbols so that shields and coats of arms were not used by more than one family. In 1484 Richard III founded the College of Arms, which now has its home in Queen Victoria Street, London.

Gradually these designs became used in the decoration of the family estate rather than on the battlefield and were a way of pointing out to visitors the distinguished pedigree of the family. Keep an eye out for coats of arms and emblems when you visit stately homes and see if you can trace how the shields have developed through the generations.

Combining forces

Shields became more complicated if a marriage took place between a man and woman who each had a family shield, as these would have to be combined to form a new one. As you can imagine, some designs became very intricate.

Little Mawtun Hall

The stained-glass windows at Little Moreton Hall in Cheshire include pictures of a wolf's head and a barrel. 'Maw' was an old English word for the jaw of a wild animal and 'tun' is another word for barrel. Put together as Mawtun these words sounded similar to the family name, Moreton. These punning puzzles are called 'rebuses'.

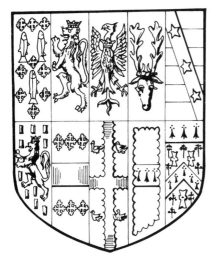

A very old coat

A whole language sprang up with heraldry based on medieval French which was the main language of the English court. This gave ample scope for punning: the Lucy family of Charlecote in Warwickshire used three pike on their shield as the heraldic term for these fish was 'lucie'.

Sir Thomas Lucy, who lived at Charlecote in the sixteenth century, was very proud of his coat of arms and his ancestors. The story goes that whenever his coat of arms was mentioned he used to reply 'and a very old coat too'. The playwright Shakespeare, who was caught and punished for poaching deer at Charlecote as a young man, got his own back by basing one of his comic characters, Justice Shallow, a pompous man obsessed with his ancestry, on Sir Thomas.

Don't step on the dog

Richard Brownlow was granted the use of the greyhound on his crest by Queen Elizabeth I in 1593. His descendant, 'Young' Sir John Brownlow, was so proud of it that it crops up all over the house which he built at Belton in Lincolnshire: you can see dogs moulded on the wrought-iron gate, etched into the doorlocks and even painted in the design on the wooden floor.

Other heraldic animals to look out for in National Trust properties:

Knole, Kent – Sackville leopards

Blickling, Norfolk – Hobart bulls

Calke Abbey, Derbyshire – Harpur boar

Castle Drogo, Devon – Drewe lion

Searching for an identity

Surnames came into use for most people in the thirteenth century, when the legal system became established and it was important to identify individuals and distinguish them from other people. In some remote parts of Britain people didn't use surnames regularly until the last century.

Before surnames became hereditary – that is, handed down from generation to generation – people used names to single them out from the rest of the community. Among other things, they could get their name through something to do with their appearance, their job or where they came from or lived.

Can you think of some more examples of surnames that you know which might fall into these categories?

Appearance	Job	Place of Origin
Redhead	Baker	London
Little	Butler	Yewbank
....	....	....
....	....	....
....	....	....
....	....	....

A person's name could change several times during his or her lifetime with this system and these were really like our nicknames. However, once surnames became hereditary, families could get stuck with a name that wasn't necessarily appropriate. You could be unlucky and be a doctor called Butcher or a very short man called Longfellow!

Franglais influences

When William I conquered England in 1066 he came with a group of Norman barons whom he rewarded for their loyalty by giving them chunks of his newly acquired land. Many of the barons were simply called by a Christian name followed by the name of their area of France, such as Richard de Courson. In time these French place names became adapted to form surnames. Richard de Courson's descendants are the Curzons of Kedleston in Derbyshire. Until the late Middle Ages French was the language of the English court and French words slipped into the language, so some surnames are from French words that have been altered over the years to English spelling. Here are some examples:

Pettigrew comes from petit cru – small growth, ie. short

Bellamy comes from bel ami – good friend

David Davidson and Sons

Before names became fixed men would often take their father's name as a type of descriptive surname. Everyone would know by his name that William Davidson was William, the son of David. This obviously changed from generation to generation, so that if William Davidson had a son called Thomas his name would be Thomas Williamson.

If your name ends with 'son' or begins with Mac or Mc, O' or Fitz, or Ap (the Scottish, Irish and Welsh versions) this means that your surname probably comes from this group and that way back in the mists of time you had an ancestor who had part of your surname as his first name.

Multi-barrelled surnames

If you thought that was confusing, try the traditional Muslim way where the father takes the name of his eldest son and adds it to his own list of descendants, going back at least three generations. The family of the Duke of Buckingham, who owned Stowe in Buckinghamshire, used a similar idea: his name was Richard Temple-Nugent-Brydges-Chandos-Grenville!

International flavour

Your family may have come to live in Britain quite recently, or perhaps they settled here from another country over hundreds of years ago. Each race, culture and religion has its traditional system of naming. Here are just a few examples from the many different cultures living in Britain today.

Jewish custom

Some Jews also took their father or mother's first name as a surname and added the words 'Ben' or 'Bar' meaning 'son of' or 'daughter of'. However, Jews have settled in all parts of the world, and usually take on the naming system of the country they have made their home.

Religious refugees

In some cases Jews have come to England to escape persecution, although at times they have also been driven out of England for the same reason. England was also a refuge in the seventeenth century for Huguenots – or French Protestants – who fled across the Channel from the Catholic regime. Many were skilled craftsmen who set up successful businesses. Huguenot names, like Bosanquet, are still found today, little changed from the seventeenth century.

Chinese clans

The Chinese have a great sense of family identity, and this is shown through the traditional naming system. Chinese people usually have a three-part name: first comes the 'clan' name or surname; then the generation name and lastly a personal name eg. Wong Meng Yeong.

Lost histories

Until slavery was abolished in the nineteenth century, thousands of Africans were captured and shipped to the West Indies and the Americas to work on the plantations. It is difficult for the people descended from these slaves to trace their family history back to Africa. When slaves are mentioned in written records they are often referred to by first names given to them by their employer, and when they were freed many took on the name of the plantation where they had worked or the ship by which they had arrived. None of these gave any trace of their African roots.

If the name Fitz

Charles II who ruled England from 1660 to 1685 had many, many lovers and as a consequence, many children. Some say he was a father to over seventy! A large number of these took the surname Fitzroy which means 'son of the king' ('roi' is French for 'king').

What's in a name?

First names can be just as interesting as surnames and hereditary in their own way. You may be named after a relative or have one of your parent's names or even a family surname as a middle name. Names go in and out of fashion and parents sometimes name children after current film or television stars or royalty. Fanatic football supporters have even been known to name their child after an entire team!

Montacute, Somerset

Florence and Parthenope Nightingale

Florence Nightingale, who saved many lives in the Crimean War through introducing basic hygiene to the battlefield hospitals, was named after her birthplace in Italy. Her sister, who lived at Claydon House in Buckinghamshire, had an even more exotic name, Parthenope, which was the alternative name for Naples, the Italian city where she had been born. It's lucky Mrs Nightingale didn't give birth in Leighton Buzzard or Bognor Regis!

Philip XIV....

Just as belongings can be handed down from generation to generation so, too, can names. From 1733 to 1978 the owners of Erddig in North Wales were either called Philip or Simon Yorke, while from 1586 to 1753 the eldest sons of the Phelips family from Montacute in Somerset were always called Edward. Some families stuck very strictly to this rule and if the eldest boy died as a baby, the next male would be given the same name to keep the tradition alive.

The Proud Duke

Charles Seymour, the 6th Duke of Somerset, who also lived at Petworth, was known as the Proud Duke. He had such a high opinion of his standing that he copied the way that some oriental monarchs kept themselves apart from the masses. He believed that he would be corrupted if ordinary mortals looked at him and so he got footmen to run ahead of his carriage to clear people away from the path.

Nicknames

Some people lose their first name altogether and get stuck with extraordinary nicknames, for example 'Capability' Brown, the famous landscape designer who got his nickname because he often told his clients that their gardens had 'capabilities'.

Royal nicknames

Before surnames came into common use, descriptive nicknames were often a way of distinguishing the person. Many of the examples which have survived belong to rulers, but are not as straightforward as you might think. Can you work out how the following got their nicknames?

Ethelred the Unready

Richard the Lionheart

Harold Harefoot

Ivan the Terrible

Edward the Martyr

Edmund Ironside

Bloody Mary

The Black Prince

Philip the Fair

James of the Fiery Face

Answers on page 32

The Wizard Earl

Henry Percy, 9th Earl of Northumberland and owner of Petworth in Sussex, was locked up in the Tower of London for sixteen years suspected of involvement in the Gunpowder Plot, when a group of Catholics attempted to blow up the Houses of Parliament. He was released in 1621 and spent the rest of his life at Petworth carrying out scientific experiments and as a result was known as 'The Wizard Earl'.

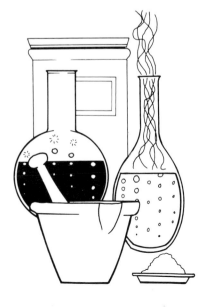

What about me?

Go to your local library and ask if they have a dictionary of British surnames. If you have a British name, you should be able to find it listed and the background behind it. You can do the same with your first name too.

Marriage makers

Arranged marriages were common in Britain in the Middle Ages as they were a means of accumulating wealth and power. It was not unusual for children to be engaged or betrothed before their tenth birthday.

Starting young

When her father died in 1670, Elizabeth Percy was only three years old but was a big stake in the marriage game as she was heiress to vast family estates which included Petworth in Sussex. By her sixteenth birthday she had been married three times! Her first husband, whom she married when she was thirteen, died the following year; her next husband was killed by her lover in 1682 and later in the year she was married to the 6th Duke of Somerset (the Proud Duke, see page 11). This marriage lasted slightly longer for forty years until Elizabeth's death in 1722.

Keeping it in the family

Dame Alice Brownlow of Belton had seven children, although only five daughters survived to adulthood. Her husband died in 1697 when the girls were still young and it became Alice's mission to secure the best possible marriages. She was very successful: two married earls and one a duke. The third daughter, Margaret, died of smallpox a few days before her wedding to Lord Willoughby but Alice's match did not go to waste as Jane, the fourth daughter, took her place a few months later. The youngest daughter, Eleanor, married a cousin, as her mother had done and so once again the estate remained in the family.

Dame Alice's memorial in Belton parish church notes her matchmaking skills: 'having five young daughters left to her care she was chiefly employed in their education; three of them she disposed in marriage to three noble Peers of this realm and the fourth to her husband's nephew out of respect to his memory'.

Belton

Marrying into royalty

Frederick Hervey, the eccentric 4th Earl of Bristol who lived at Ickworth in Suffolk, wasn't quite as successful in matchmaking. In 1796 he tried to marry off his eldest son to an illegitimate daughter of the King of Prussia because it would bring '£5,000 a year, besides a principality in Germany, an English Dukedom for Frederick or me ... a perpetual relationship with both the Princess of Wales and her children ... the Embassy to Berlin'. Frederick ended up marrying his true love, an Irish girl, and the Earl stayed dukedomless.

Matchmaker supreme

Bess of Hardwick was extremely skilled in arranging advantageous marriages ... for herself! She managed to rise from being a daughter of a Derbyshire squire, with an inheritance of £26, to one of the wealthiest women in sixteenth-century England through marrying four times – each time to someone richer and higher up the social ladder. After the death of her last and wealthiest husband, the Earl of Shrewsbury, she built Hardwick Hall in Derbyshire, possibly the grandest house of the age.

Hardwick Hall, Derbyshire

Countess AND Duchess

Some people always wanted a little more. In 1769 the scheming wife of the 3rd Earl of Bristol became a duchess by marrying the Duke of Kingston. The only hiccough was that she was still married to her first husband, the Earl ... When this was discovered, it was one of the greatest scandals of the century.

Uppark Dairy, Sussex

Mix and match

Although many kings, princes and nobles had mistresses from all levels of society – like Charles II's favourite orange seller, Nell Gwynn – they rarely married them and chose a wife from their own class. Some marriages were more unusual. In 1792 Sir Henry Harpur of Calke Abbey, Derbyshire married a lady's maid, Nanette Hawkins, while in 1825 Sir Harry Fetherstonhaugh, the elderly owner of Uppark in Sussex, married his teenage dairymaid, Mary Ann Bullock.

Inheritance and illegitimacy

By English law, hereditary titles had to pass to the eldest son, or failing that, the closest male relative. If the relative had a different surname it was common for him to change his name on inheriting the title so that continuity of the family name and survival of the line would be certain. This is exactly what happened in the Brownlow family of Belton House in Lincolnshire: the family name has been added to another surname in some cases to keep the line going. However, unless the property was 'entailed' or linked to the title, it could be left to whomever the owner named in the Will. This means that Wills often show the whim of the individual: there are even tales of millionaires leaving all their money to their favourite pets.

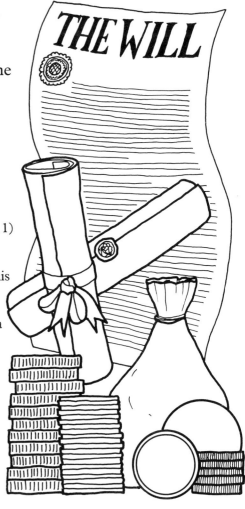

Women only

Wills can affect generations to come. Mary Parminter, who with her cousin, Jane, built A la Ronde – an eighteenth-century octagonal house in Devon – declared in her Will that the house should only be handed down through unmarried women in the family. Until the National Trust took on the house in 1991 there had only ever been one male owner.

Caught dozing

Charles Seymour, 6th Duke of Somerset, was so proud (see page 11) that he always wore full regalia around the house and insisted that his children remained standing in his presence. He cut £20,000 off the inheritance of his daughter, Charlotte, when he woke up from a cat-nap to find her sitting down in his presence!

A la Ronde, Devon

Better late than never

The 3rd Earl of Egremont of Petworth in Sussex had six children before he married their mother in 1801. This meant that the children, being born 'out of wedlock', were declared illegitimate. As a result Lord Egremont's title passed to a nephew, but his eldest son was left the house and estates.

Heirless

The estate of Knole in Kent is entailed, which means that before it came into the ownership of the National Trust in 1946, it had to pass through the male line. Thus, although Vita Sackville-West was descended on both her mother's and her father's side from Thomas Sackville and felt desperately attached to Knole, the estate passed to her uncle on her father's death.

Sarah-Anne Child

Change of plan

Robert Child, the wealthy eighteenth-century banker who lived at Osterley House in Middlesex, had just one child, a headstrong girl called Sarah-Anne. She greatly upset him by falling in love with the unpredictable 10th Earl of Westmorland, known as 'Rapid Westmorland', and running away to get married in a pub in Gretna Green. Robert made a new Will and left most of his fortune and Osterley to Sarah-Anne's second son or eldest daughter to make sure that his son-in-law and future Earls of Westmorland didn't gain from the love match. As Robert had wished, Osterley passed to Lady Sophia Fane, Lady Westmorland's eldest daughter.

Knole, Kent

Name change

Sir William Blackett of Wallington in Northumberland died in 1728, leaving only an illegitimate daughter, Elizabeth Ord. In order to make sure her future was secure, he stated in his Will that his nephew, Walter Calverley, would inherit the property and title on the condition that he married Elizabeth and changed his name to Blackett, which he did. There was another blip in the Wallington succession in 1879 when the 6th baronet, Walter Trevelyan, died childless. The next in line was Sir Walter's Catholic nephew, of whom he disapproved for religious reasons. So, although the title and the Nettlecombe estate which was linked to the title went to this heir, Sir Walter left the Wallington estate in to his cousin, Charles Edward Trevelyan.

Home sweet home

How many times has your family moved house? People move around a great deal now, travelling to different parts of the country or even abroad with their work and are not tied to one place as in the past. Many of the families in National Trust homes lived in the same house, or at least on the same site, for centuries and the houses were built specifically for the family. You will therefore often see clues to the ownership in the actual construction of the house: look out for initials, family crests and coats of arms on the building both inside and outside.

Initial impressions

We've already seen how heraldry features in house decoration. The following houses show some of the other ways people chose to leave their mark on their homes for generations to come:

Blickling Hall, Norfolk: Henry Hobart had his initials and those of his family moulded on the lead drainpipes when the house was built in 1625.

Beningbrough Hall, Yorkshire: John and Mary Bourchier's initials are inlaid in the wooden floor of the stair landing, along with two knots – the badge of the family – and the date 1716 when the house was built.

Trerice, Cornwall: The plasterwork ceiling panel in the Hall includes the initials of Sir John Arundell, his first wife, Katherine, and his sister, Margaret.

Hardwick Hall, Derbyshire: Bess of Hardwick must win the prize for making her mark. This impressive Elizabethan woman made sure people could be in no doubt as to who built Hardwick Hall: she had her initials 'ES' for Elizabeth Shrewsbury carved in enormous stone letters along the roof-top.

Not so brief ...

Other builders have been more wordy. At Little Moreton Hall in Cheshire, William Moreton was so proud of his new home that he asked the carpenter to carve 'made by William Moreton in the yeare of our Lorde MDLIX' above the windows in the main courtyard.

Little Moreton Hall, Cheshire

A Jekyll and Hyde house

Often the overall design of a house gives a clue to the people who built it. The best example of this is Castle Ward in Co. Down, Northern Ireland, a house with a split personality! It was built in the 1770s when the Gothic style of architecture was in fashion. Bernard Ward, the owner of the estate, preferred the classical style, but his wife, Lady Anne, was determined to have an up-to-date Gothic house. Neither would give in so they met half way ... literally. One half of the house was built to a classical design with a pediment, square headed windows, and columns, while the other half of the house had pointed windows, a crenellated balustrade and pinnacles. The division even carried through to the inside decoration.

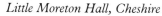

Castle Ward, Co. Down

An old look

Penrhyn Castle in North Wales might look old from the outside but it was, in fact, built in the 1830s to look like an eleventh-century stronghold.

17

Every picture tells a story

Visit practically any National Trust furnished house and you'll find pictures of people connected with the property. Portraits are an excellent way of tracing family history. Formal portraits were often painted to give some clue to the character, interests or occupation of the sitter.

The Artist

Richard, 2nd Baron Edgcumbe, the eighteenth-century owner of Cotehele in Cornwall, was a talented artist, and portraits of him as a small child and as a grown man show him holding an artist's crayon.

The Improver

The eighteenth-century portrait of Richard Pennant, owner of the huge Penrhyn estate in North Wales, shows him with his hand on a map, pointing out the new road which he constructed on his land – one of the many improvements he carried out.

The Enthusiast

Frederick Hervey, the 4th Earl of Bristol, spent more time out of England than in it. He was fascinated by life on the Continent and Italy in particular, where he lived for many years studying art and architecture. A portrait of him at the family home of Ickworth, Suffolk shows him in front of Vesuvius, the volcano which he used to climb daily when he stayed in Naples.

More than meets the eye

Some pictures have even more to say. At Kedleston in Derbyshire is a painting telling the story of the family of Nathaniel Curzon, the 4th Baronet. It shows him and his wife Mary holding their second baby son, Nathaniel, while they are being watched from the clouds by John, their first born who died, aged one, in 1720. This would have been painted to celebrate the birth of a healthy male heir.

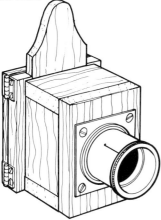

The camera never lies ...

Since the invention of photography 150 years ago we have a more accurate record of what people looked like. It was also more affordable for people to have a photograph taken rather than commission an artist.

Timely alterations

Paintings were sometimes altered to reflect sadder times. A portrait of Lady Elizabeth Hardwicke at Wimpole in Cambridgeshire, which was originally painted in 1782, had a black dress daubed over the Countess's light-coloured clothes in 1810, after both her sons had died within a couple of years of each other. In the twentieth century the portrait was cleaned and restored to its original state.

Lacock Abbey, Wiltshire

Say cheese!

In the early days of photography people treated having their photo taken very seriously. If you're looking round a house and see any old photographs it's a pretty safe bet that no-one will be smiling. It took a lot longer to take a photograph so it would have been difficult to hold a grin for any length of time.

William Fox Talbot invented the photographic negative: he took the first photograph to be developed from a negative in 1835 of a small oriel window at his family home of Lacock Abbey in Wiltshire.

Have you or your family got some old photograph albums? They will tell you a lot about your family history.

Upstairs, downstairs

G rand houses would have ground to a halt had it not been for the armies of servants behind the scenes, cooking the food, cleaning the house, tending the gardens and looking after the horses. Although you can see how servants lived and worked in many National Trust houses, usually there are few records of the names of these crucial people or pictures of what they looked like.

There is one amazing exception – Erddig in North Wales. The Yorke family, who lived at Erddig from the 1700s, were devoted to their servants and even composed poems about them and had their portraits painted or photographs taken. Thanks to them we have a record of the servants' names, what they did, their characters and what they looked like. Here are just a couple of extracts from the poems:

Mary Webster - cook
'Upon the portly frame we look
Of one who was our former Cook.
No better keeper of our Store,
Did ever enter at our door.'

Sarah Davies - dairymaid
'In everything she did well please
Save in the art of making cheese.'

Identity crisis
John Jones (tho' not alone), the same!
Our Coachman also bears that name:
'Tis one well known midst hills and dales
Of this our famous land of Wales
A third yet answers to our call,
At this time dwelling at our Hall
We in our household once had five,
And others still might be alive.'

Housekeeper and tour guide
At Kedleston Hall in Derbyshire there is a portrait of Mrs Garnett, the housekeeper from 1766 to 1809, who is shown holding a book with the title **Catalogue of Pictures, Statues, &c**. It would have been part of her job to give people a tour of the house if the Curzon family were away and she would have used this as her reference book.

Collections

Nearly everyone's home has its special character and different rooms can tell you about certain personalities. You probably decorate your bedroom with posters of your favourite pop stars or sports players – people in the past also filled their houses with objects that show their particular interests.

Tatton Park, Cheshire

The 4th Lord Egerton was a keen big game hunter and travelled to Africa and India on hunting expeditions. He shot so many animals that a new hall was built for the sole purpose of displaying his stuffed trophies.

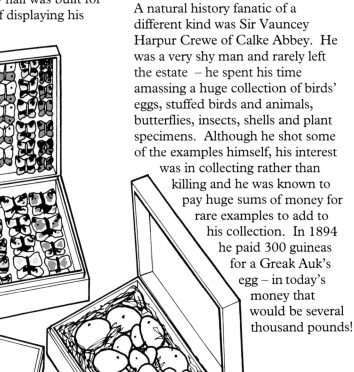

Calke Abbey, Derbyshire

A natural history fanatic of a different kind was Sir Vauncey Harpur Crewe of Calke Abbey. He was a very shy man and rarely left the estate – he spent his time amassing a huge collection of birds' eggs, stuffed birds and animals, butterflies, insects, shells and plant specimens. Although he shot some of the examples himself, his interest was in collecting rather than killing and he was known to pay huge sums of money for rare examples to add to his collection. In 1894 he paid 300 guineas for a Greak Auk's egg – in today's money that would be several thousand pounds!

Snowshill Manor, Gloucestershire

Charles Wade was a collector extraordinaire. He bought Snowshill Manor in 1919 as a place to house his collection of objects which range from Japanese armour to doll's houses, with a lot in between. The house was so full of his possessions that he had to live in a cottage in the garden!

Paper, paper - read all about it

How often do you write letters? How often do you use the telephone? With modern technology the telephone has replaced the letter as the common form of communication and fewer and fewer people write letters. However, for the past five hundred years writing has been the main means of communication between people and luckily many of these letters and documents have survived. Documents often deal with day-to-day affairs but journals and diaries give us fascinating insights into people's characters and relationships.

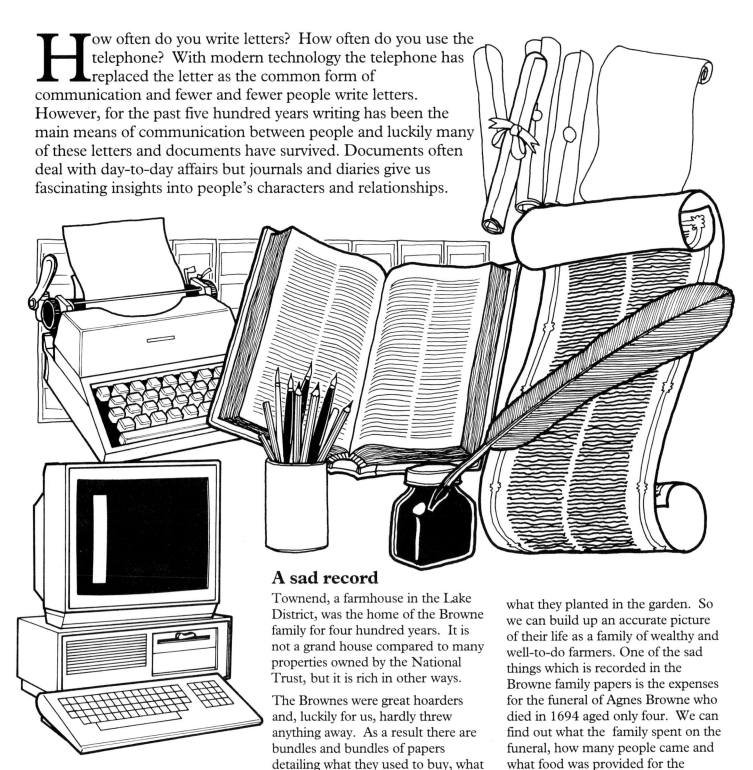

A sad record

Townend, a farmhouse in the Lake District, was the home of the Browne family for four hundred years. It is not a grand house compared to many properties owned by the National Trust, but it is rich in other ways.

The Brownes were great hoarders and, luckily for us, hardly threw anything away. As a result there are bundles and bundles of papers detailing what they used to buy, what they sold, what they spent and even what they planted in the garden. So we can build up an accurate picture of their life as a family of wealthy and well-to-do farmers. One of the sad things which is recorded in the Browne family papers is the expenses for the funeral of Agnes Browne who died in 1694 aged only four. We can find out what the family spent on the funeral, how many people came and what food was provided for the mourners to eat.

Every last detail

It is much more common for record books to have survived from the households of the aristocracy. These books were kept by a steward who would record every expense from buying new clothes for the servants to paying a famous artist for a portrait of the owner of the house. In the eighteenth century, when many wealthy young men went abroad to Europe on a 'Grand Tour' to study classical sites, we have the steward to thank for giving a full picture of the places visited and objects bought by the young master.

Sir George Lucy of Charlecote Park in Warwickshire was one such adventurer, and the places that he visited and things that he bought have been carefully recorded by his housekeeper.

Samplers

The first samplers were just that - samples of different kinds of embroidery stitch. They became extremely popular in the eighteenth and nineteenth centuries when as part of their schooling girls would embroider pieces of cloth: sometimes with religious texts or even names of the members of the family and birthdates on a background decorated with stitches. What makes them interesting is that the embroiderer would always 'sign' the work, sewing her name and age along with the date of the sampler.

The family bible

Couples were often given a family bible when they got married. In the front of this they wrote down the history of their close family with dates of birth, marriages and death. This in turn got handed down from generation to generation, giving a compact run down of important dates. You could find out if you have a family bible.

Ashes to ashes

For centuries people have respected the dead and usually mark their graves with a stone or, if they were from a wealthy family, an ornate tomb complete with sculpture. The simplest memorials give the person's name, age and date of death but others give a summary of the deceased's life.

Many stately homes, like The Vyne in Hampshire, have private chapels with memorials to members of the family through the ages. Memorials are not necessarily at the place where the body is buried and were often erected by descendants long after the person had died as a mark of respect and honour.

Tomb Chamber

In 1770 John Chute decided to give over a whole room in his house, The Vyne, to the honour of his distinguished seventeenth-century ancestor, Challoner Chute, who had been Speaker of the House of Commons. He paid for an elaborate marble sculpture of the Speaker and on the base is a list of the descendants showing how John Chute was related to Challoner Chute. The room is called the Tomb Chamber.

Murder most foul

Westminster Abbey in London is packed full of fascinating tombs and memorials, including that of Thomas Thynne of Longleat, who was the unfortunate second husband of Elizabeth Percy, the wealthy teenage heiress to Petworth (see page 12). In 1682 he was murdered by assassins hired by his wife's lover, and his memorial features a carved panel showing the scene of his murder in Pall Mall, London where his coach was ambushed. The inscription doesn't beat about the bush: 'Barbarously Murdered on Sunday the 12th of February 1682'.

Newton's memorial

Tombs could also show the particular interests of the dead person. Sir Isaac Newton, the famous seventeenth-century scientist who was born at Woolsthorpe Manor in Lincolnshire, is remembered in a tomb in Westminster Abbey decorated with cherubs playing with telescopes and other scientific instruments. ▶

The Bookworm

The memorial in Charlecote Church, Warwickshire to the third Sir Thomas Lucy who died in 1640, includes a shelf of books carved in marble showing his interest in the arts: he was a friend of the poet John Donne.

The Improver

The monument to Richard Pennant in Llandygai church includes a quarryman, a peasant girl and three carved scenes showing what improvements he had made to his North Wales Penrhyn estate in education, agriculture and slate quarrying. ▼

In a word ...

However lifelike the sculpture was, it was often up to the inscription to give some idea of the person's actual character. According to his epitaph – the words written on a memorial – Sir John Harpur Crewe, the owner of Calke Abbey in Derbyshire, was 'averse to public life and spent the greater part of his days at Calke among his own people, doing good to all around him'.

Family monuments

When Nathaniel Curzon was planning his grand new stately home on his Derbyshire estate in the 1750s, he decided to relocate the village of Kedleston but to leave the twelfth-century village church where it was. The church was the burial place of many of his ancestors and Nathaniel was obviously proud of his long family history, which dated back to the Norman Conquest in 1066.

Kedleston Church is a good place to see how the style of memorials has changed over the centuries. Here are a few of the main monuments which you can see there in memory of various members of the Curzon family. If you had a choice, what sort of memorial would you like to be remembered by?

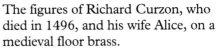

An oblong slab with a carved cross which dates back to the thirteenth century and might be in memory of Thomas de Curzon who died in 1245.

A monument erected in 1906 by the heartbroken George Nathaniel Curzon to his first wife Mary, who died at the age of thirty-six. The resting figures of the Marquess and his wife are carved in white Italian marble on top of a marble tomb chest.

The figures of Richard Curzon, who died in 1496, and his wife Alice, on a medieval floor brass.

A large monument featuring Sir Nathaniel, the 2nd Baronet, and his wife, Sarah Penn. It was put up by their youngest daughter, Jane, in 1737, eighteen years after her father's death.

A memorial on the wall with the three-quarter length figures of Sir John Curzon, 1st Baronet, and his wife Patience which was put up in 1664, twenty-two years before Sir John died! Beneath their figures are three-quarter length carvings of their children.

Look for more

Although Kedleston is unusual in having so many memorials to the same family, if you visit an old parish church you should be able to find a good range of monuments inside and headstones in the graveyard. You may need some help reading some of the dates as they are often in Roman numerals.

You may have your own family tombs or gravestones in a local churchyard. See if you can find out where your ancestors are buried.

A detailed carving above William Curzon's memorial tablet. He died in the Battle of Waterloo in 1815. The carved bird appears on several other tombs in the church.

Rub a dub dub

If you visit a church and find an interesting floor brass or slab, ask the vicar if you can take a rubbing from it. You'll need a wax crayon and a large sheet of paper. Place the sheet of paper over the stone or brass and then, using the crayon on its side, rub evenly over the whole area until you have the image of the memorial on your paper.

A tale of two families

The Curzons of Kedleston

Look at this family tree and follow the Curzons through twenty-eight generations to the present day. Can you match the people mentioned in the memorials on pages 26 and 27 with the ones on this family tree?

CURZON OF KEDLESTON

Names in **bold** type indicate the line of male descent.
The broken line indicates illegitimate children.

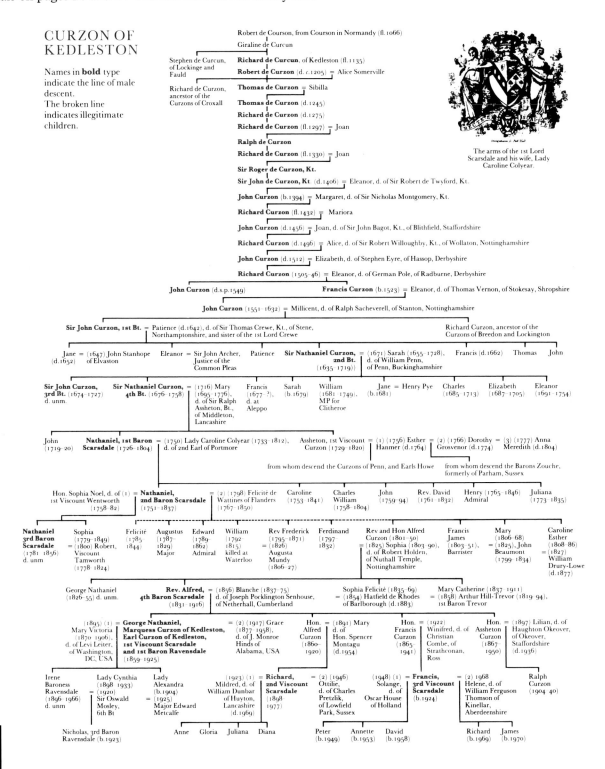

The arms of the 1st Lord Scarsdale and his wife, Lady Caroline Colyear.

Robert de Courson, from Courson in Normandy (fl.1066)

Giraline de Curcun

Stephen de Curcun, of Locking and Fauld

Richard de Curcun, of Kedleston (fl.1135)

Richard de Curzon, ancestor of the Curzons of Croxall

Robert de Curzon (d.c.1205) = Alice Somerville

Thomas de Curzon = Sibilla

Thomas de Curzon (d.1245)

Richard de Curzon (d.1275)

Richard de Curzon (fl.1297) = Joan

Ralph de Curzon

Richard de Curzon (fl.1330) = Joan

Sir Roger de Curzon, Kt.

Sir John de Curzon, Kt. (d.1406) = Eleanor, d. of Sir Robert de Twyford, Kt.

John Curzon (b.1394) = Margaret, d. of Sir Nicholas Montgomery, Kt.

Richard Curzon (fl.1432) = Mariora

John Curzon (d.1456) = Joan, d. of Sir John Bagot, Kt., of Blithfield, Staffordshire

Richard Curzon (d.1496) = Alice, d. of Sir Robert Willoughby, Kt., of Wollaton, Nottinghamshire

John Curzon (d.1512) = Elizabeth, d. of Stephen Eyre, of Hassop, Derbyshire

Richard Curzon (1505-46) = Eleanor, d. of German Pole, of Radburne, Derbyshire

John Curzon (d.s.p.1549)

Francis Curzon (b.1523) = Eleanor, d. of Thomas Vernon, of Stokesay, Shropshire

John Curzon (1551-1632) = Millicent, d. of Ralph Sacheverell, of Stanton, Nottinghamshire

Sir John Curzon, 1st Bt. = Patience (d.1642), d. of Sir Thomas Crewe, Kt., of Stene, Northamptonshire, and sister of the 1st Lord Crewe

Richard Curzon, ancestor of the Curzons of Breedon and Lockington

Jane (d.1652) = (1647) John Stanhope of Elvaston

Eleanor = Sir John Archer, Justice of the Common Pleas

Patience

Sir Nathaniel Curzon, 2nd Bt. (1635-1719) = (1671) Sarah (1655-1728), d. of William Penn, of Penn, Buckinghamshire

Francis (d.1662)

Thomas

John

Sir John Curzon, 3rd Bt. (1674-1727) d. unm.

Sir Nathaniel Curzon, 4th Bt. (1676-1758) = (1716) Mary (1695-1776), d. of Sir Ralph Assheton, Bt., of Middleton, Lancashire

Francis (1677-?), d. at Aleppo

Sarah (b.1679)

William (1681-1749), MP for Clitheroe

Jane (b.1681) = Henry Pye

Charles (1685-1713)

Elizabeth (1687-1705)

Eleanor (1691-1754)

John (1719-20)

Nathaniel, 1st Baron Scarsdale (1726-1804) = (1750) Lady Caroline Colyear (1733-1812), d. of 2nd Earl of Portmore

Assheton, 1st Viscount Curzon (1729-1820) = (1) (1756) Esther Hanmer (d.1764) = (2) (1766) Dorothy Grosvenor (d.1774) = (3) (1777) Anna Meredith (d.1804)

from whom descend the Curzons of Penn, and Earls Howe

from whom descend the Barons Zouche, formerly of Parham, Sussex

Hon. Sophia Noel, d. of (1) = **Nathaniel, 2nd Baron Scarsdale** (1751-1837) = (2) (1798) Felicité de Wattines of Flanders (1767-1850)
1st Viscount Wentworth (1758-82)

Caroline (1753-1841)

Charles William (1758-1804)

John (1759-94)

Rev. David (1761-1832)

Henry (1765-1846) Admiral

Juliana (1773-1835)

Nathaniel 3rd Baron Scarsdale (1781-1856) d. unm

Sophia (1779-1849) = (1800) Robert, Viscount Tamworth (1778-1824)

Felicité (1785-1844)

Augustus (1787-1829) Major

Edward (1789-1862) Admiral

William (1792-1815) killed at Waterloo

Rev Frederick (1795-1871) = (1826) Augusta Mundy (1806-27)

Ferdinand (1797-1832)

Rev and Hon Alfred Curzon (1801-50) = (1825) Sophia (1803-90), d. of Robert Holden, of Nuthall Temple, Nottinghamshire

Francis James (1803-51), Barrister

Mary (1806-68) = (1825), John Beaumont (1799-1834)

Caroline Esther (1808-86) = (1827) William Drury-Lowe (d.1877)

George Nathaniel (1826-55) d. unm.

Rev. Alfred, 4th Baron Scarsdale (1831-1916) = (1856) Blanche (1837-75), d. of Joseph Pocklington Senhouse, of Netherhall, Cumberland

Sophia Felicité (1835-69) = (1854) Hatfield de Rhodes, of Barlborough (d.1883)

Mary Catherine (1837-1911) = (1858) Arthur Hill-Trevor (1819-94), 1st Baron Trevor

(1895) (1) Mary Victoria (1870-1906), d. of Levi Leiter, of Washington, DC, USA = **George Nathaniel, Marquess Curzon of Kedleston, Earl Curzon of Kedleston, 1st Viscount Scarsdale and 1st Baron Ravensdale** (1859-1925) = (2) (1917) Grace (1877-1958), d. of J. Monroe Hinds of Alabama, USA

Hon. Alfred Curzon (1860-1920) = (1891) Mary d. of Hon. Spencer Montagu (d.1954)

Hon. Francis Curzon (1865-1941) = (1922) Winifred, d. of Christian Combe, of Strathconan, Ross

Hon. Assheton Curzon (1867-1950) = (1897) Lilian, d. of Haughton Okeover, of Okeover, Staffordshire (d.1936)

Irene Baroness Ravensdale (1896-1966) d. unm

Lady Cynthia (1898-1933) = (1920) Sir Oswald Mosley, 6th Bt.

Lady Alexandra (b.1904) = (1925) Major Edward Metcalfe

(1923) (1) Mildred, d. of William Dunbar of Huyton, Lancashire (d.1969) = **Richard, 2nd Viscount Scarsdale** (1898-1977) = (2) (1946) Ottilie, d. of Charles Pretzlik, of Lowfield Park, Sussex

(1948) (1) Solange, d. of Oscar House of Holland = **Francis, 3rd Viscount Scarsdale** (b.1924) = (2) 1968 Helene, d. of William Ferguson Thomson of Kinellar, Aberdeenshire

Ralph Curzon (1904-40)

Nicholas, 3rd Baron Ravensdale (b.1923)

Anne Gloria Juliana Diana

Peter (b.1949) Annette (b.1953) David (b.1958)

Richard (b.1969) James (b.1970)

28

The Butcher family tree

Look at the diagram below and compare it with the Curzon tree. This is the family tree which has been traced so far of the Butcher family who made their living cutting peat on Wicken Fen in Cambridgeshire. Although this tree only goes back over five generations, it has taken a great deal of research through parish records and census returns to piece it together. There are no paintings of the ancestors but some photos survive from each traced generation. All we know of earlier generations is that one ancestor must have been involved in the meat trade for the family to have the surname Butcher.

The Butcher and Curzon families were poles apart in wealth but some things affected all classes: they had large families, but often children didn't reach adulthood and tragedies could strike regardless of wealth.

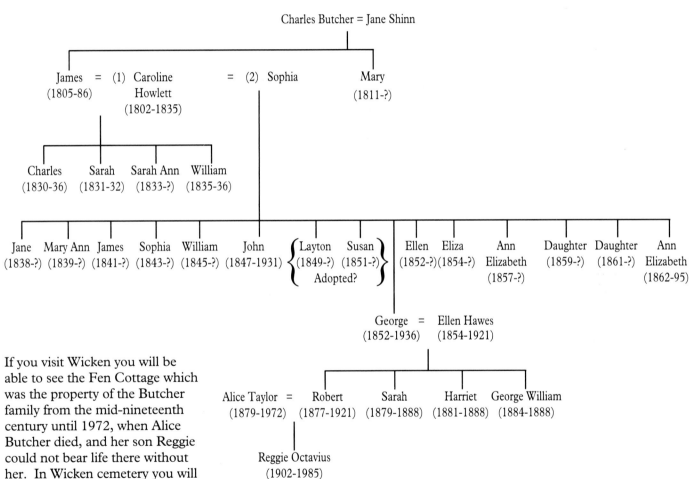

If you visit Wicken you will be able to see the Fen Cottage which was the property of the Butcher family from the mid-nineteenth century until 1972, when Alice Butcher died, and her son Reggie could not bear life there without her. In Wicken cemetery you will find the headstones of Robert Butcher, his wife, Alice, and their son, Reggie. There is a spelling mistake on Reggie's stone because the engraver could not spell Octavius, his middle name. The unmarked grave of Sarah, Harriet and George, three of George Butcher's children who died from diphtheria, is covered with daffodils in the spring.

What about me?

Now that you've read about other people's family histories, why not try to find out more about your own?

Some starting points

Collect:

Pictures or photos of family members
Pictures of their homes

Who to ask:

Your mother or father
Aunts and uncles
Grandparents
Great-grandparents

Find out:

What country your mother or father and grandparents were born in
How they met
Why they moved from place to place
What education they had
If there is a family bible or other record
What they did for a living
Where they went on holiday
How they travelled
Where your ancestors were buried

Find out as much as you can about the day-to-day life of your grandparents when they were your age and compare it with your own. Ask them where they were during the Second World War and how it affected their lives. Ask a parent what they wish they'd known about their own grandparents and then ask your grandparents the same question. You may be very lucky and have a great grandparent still alive: find out as much as you can from them before it's too late. If you have a step-parent, find out about their family too.

Once you think that you have collected enough information, put it together to make your own family album. You can keep on adding to this over the years.

A family circle

One way of showing your immediate descendants is to fill in this circle chart, or draw your own chart on a larger piece of paper. In each section write down as much information about each person as you can.

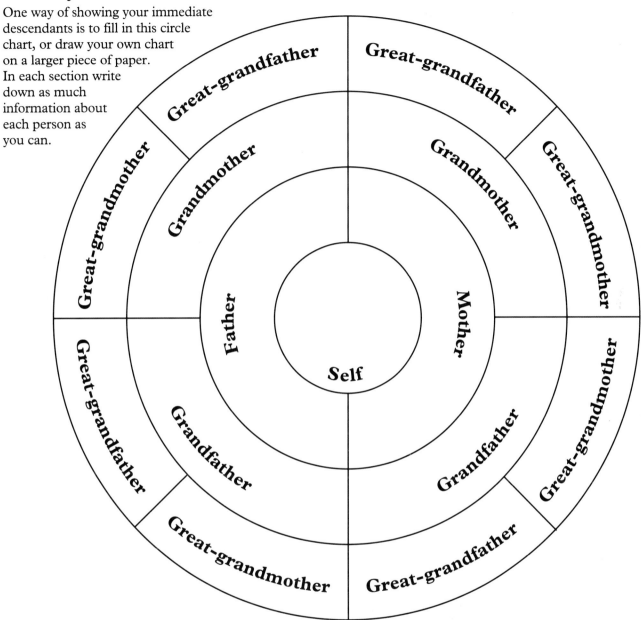

If you're interested in tracking back further in your family history there are societies and organisations to help point you in the right direction:

Federation of Family History Societies,
96 Beaumont Street, Milehouse,
Plymouth, Devon PL2 3AQ

The Society of Genealogists,
14 Charterhouse Buildings,
London EC1M 7BA

Your local library should also be able to give you information on local records and where to start looking. Remember that your best sources of information are your living relatives so don't forget to find out as much as you can from them before burying your head in books and official records.

Answers

page 11

Royal Nicknames

Ethelred the Unready
Ethelred (978-1016) wasn't unprepared: his nickname comes from the Anglo-Saxon word, 'unraed' meaning 'having no counsel' or 'foolish'.

Richard the Lionheart
Famous for his bravery in the Crusades (1190-92).

Harold Harefoot
Harold I of England (1037-40) was apparently a quick runner.

Ivan the Terrible
The Tsar of Russia from 1534-80 was known for his cruelty and fierce temper. He even killed his own son.

Edward the Martyr
The Anglo-Saxon king was murdered at Corfe Castle in Dorset in 978 by his stepmother.

Bloody Mary
The Catholic queen of England from 1553-58 was known for her fierce persecution of Protestants. During her reign she burnt alive five bishops and 300 other people for their religious beliefs.

The Black Prince
The Prince of Wales, eldest son of Edward III, was renowned for wearing a black suit of armour, but also for his campaigns in thirteenth-century France, where he left a burning trail of destruction in his path.

Philip the Fair
Philip IV, king of France from 1285-1314, was known for his good looks (but not his good deeds).

James of the Fiery Face
James II, king of Scots (1437-60) was called this because of a large red birthmark on his face.

First published in 1992 by National Trust Enterprises, 36 Queen Anne's Gate, London SW1H 9AS

Registered Charity No. 205846

ISBN   0 7078 0133 8

Designed by Blade Communications, Leamington Spa

Printed in Hong Kong by Wing King Tong